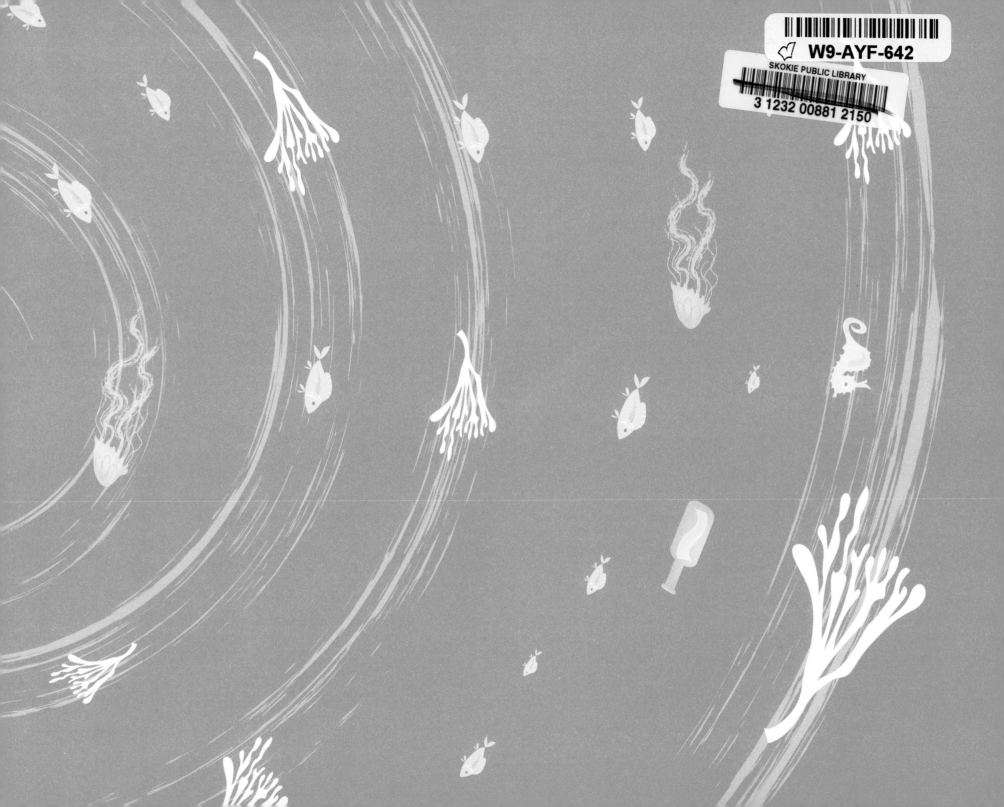

Topsy Turvy Ocean

Wes Magee • Tracey Tucker

QEB

This old octopus likes to cook and trot, but its tentacles are tied up in knots!

Tiger sharks are served
by small rainbowfish.
A squid eats spaghetti from
an oyster shell dish.

This wrecked ship that
sails on the sandy seabed
has a skeleton crew and
a captain called Fred.

This treasure chest's open.
Oh, what a surprise!
Inside there are elephants,
emus, and eyes!

Boats travel backward and glide upside down.
King Neptune is wearing a fried egg for a crown.

A deep-sea diver swims by
with a peg on her nose.
Smelly crabs and a lobster
are pinching her toes!

An electric eel pulls on a long spotted sock.
She looks in the mirror—and gets a huge shock!

Mermaids go shopping with their hair in buns,
as blue whales do ballet and a manta ray runs.

Sea sponges give dolphins
a bubble bath scrub.
Two swordfish read books
in a steamy hot tub.

A huge ugly monster
swallows a small boat,
but the anchor and chain
get caught in its throat.

Sea snakes and sirens live on the top floor,
but they can't get to sleep when the sea lions roar.

Who is that crying? It's a hammerhead shark!
The silly big softie's afraid of the dark!

The catfish are having their long whiskers cut
by lobsters who live in a wet wooden hut.

Giant turtles and starfish
sing songs of the sea
while narwhals applaud
and drink cups of tea.

Anglerfish from the deep
—what a strange sight—
wear false teeth and lipstick
when out for the night.

Seahorses pull chariots.
The wheels are on fire!
A great white shark swings
in an old tractor tire.

King Neptune's upset—his gold trident is bent—
so he sits down and cries in the porpoise's tent.

A sea serpent snores
in its four-poster bed.
His spotted pajamas
are colored bright red.

Killer whales are driving
the ocean's longest cars,
and seals waterski
by the light of the stars.

Flying fish and puffins are having a race.
A sailfish joins in. He's the winner! First place!

Next Steps

Rhymes are a unique way of introducing children to the imaginative potential of stories, word play, and creativity. Coupled with detailed illustrations of a wild and wonderful topsy turvy world, this book provides a springboard for children to explore their imagination and develop their own reading and writing skills.

LISTEN AND LOOK

Take some time to read the book. Look at the illustrations together. Can the children name and point to the ocean animals and what they are doing? Read the book again and see if the children can anticipate and join in with the rhyming words.

WRITE AND RHYME

The word "cars" can be found in this book. Can the children suggest words that rhyme with "cars"? For example, stars, bars, Mars, and jars! See if the children can think of how they could use these words to create a rhyming couplet. For example:

> On the road you see lots of cars.
> A spaceship zooms to planet Mars.

Ask the children to suggest rhymes for the following words in the book: king, whale, eel, crew, eyes, deep, toes, bed, and sea. Now see if they can try to create new rhyming couplets. The invented lines can then be written down to form a long poem. For example:

> It's nice to wiggle and waggle your toes.
> You sneeze when you have a cold in your nose.

> In the school play, I dressed up as a king.
> A song is something we love to sing...

WRITE AND IMAGINE

Ask the children to try writing a simple list poem about animals living in the ocean. Each line begins with a number, and the animals should be given "new" or different colors. Once they have listed the primary colors can they suggest more unusual ones. For example, tangerine, saffron, cream, or indigo. The list poem can begin like this:

> Deep in the ocean
> you will see:
> 1 red octopus,
> 2 blue crabs,
> 3 pink sharks,
> 4 orange dolphins...

Can the children reach number 10, or even 20? They can find plenty of ocean animals by looking through the book. The poem can then end with a chorus which is a repeat of line one.

> Deep in the ocean,
> deep in the ocean,
> deep in the ocean.

PAINT A PICTURE

This book has some wonderful illustrations. Why don't you illustrate your poems? The children can separate each couplet or line so there is one per page and then illustrate it to make their own little book. They could even create a front and back cover. Don't forget the barcode and price! Share the book with friends and family.

Learn and Discover

Topsy Turvy Ocean features a comical cast of ocean animals doing weird and wonderful things. But what do they do in real life? Choose your favorite illustrations in the book and discover more about that animal. Find some photographs of animals in the ocean and make a collage with facts you have discovered. For example:

- *Sea Lions* can be found in every ocean except the Atlantic Ocean. They spend most of their time in the water but they come ashore to sleep and rest. They have four flippers, which they use to walk and swim. They like to eat different fish, such as herring, mackerel, salmon, and sardines. They also eat squid and octopus.

- *Great White Sharks* are the largest predatory fish in the ocean. They have up to seven rows of 300 sharp, triangular teeth. They are blue-gray on the top part of their bodies and white on the bottom. This helps them blend in with the ocean so they can swim up and surprise their victim! They like to eat fish, sea lions, seals, and small whales.

- *Seahorses* have excellent eyesight and long thin snouts to help them hunt for food. They use their snouts to suck up food like a vacuum cleaner. Seahorses eat plankton, small fish, and shrimps. They don't have a stomach so they have to eat several times a day!

Quarto is the authority on a wide range of topics.
Quarto educates, entertains and enriches the lives of our readers—enthusiasts and lovers of hands-on living.

www.quartoknows.com

Editor: Sophie Hallam
Designer: Mike Henson

Copyright © QEB Publishing 2016

First published in the United States in 2016 by QEB Publishing, Inc.
6 Orchard
Lake Forest, CA 92630

A CIP record for this book is available from the Library of Congress.

ISBN 978 1 60992 999 2

Printed in China